WORLD WAR II
RESISTANCE
FIGHTERS

Matt Doeden

Lerner Publications ◆ Minneapolis

Content consultant: Eric Juhnke, Professor of History, Briar Cliff University

Lerner Publications Company
A division of Lerner Publishing Group, Inc.
241 First Avenue North
Minneapolis, MN 55401 USA

For reading levels and more information, look up this title at www.lernerbooks.com.

Library of Congress Cataloging-in-Publication Data

Names: Doeden, Matt, author.
Title: World War II resistance fighters / by Matt Doeden.
Description: Minneapolis : Lerner Publications, [2018] | Series: Heroes of World
    War II | Includes bibliographical references and index. | Audience: Grades
    4–6. | Audience: Ages 8–12.
Identifiers: LCCN 2017010790 (print) | LCCN 2017011941 (ebook) |
    ISBN 9781512498196 (eb pdf) | ISBN 9781512486414 (lb : alk. paper)
Subjects: LCSH: Anti-Nazi movement—History—20th century—Juvenile
    literature. | Anti-Nazi movement—Europe—Biography—Juvenile
    literature. | Holocaust, Jewish (1939–1945)—Juvenile literature. | Germany—
    History—1933–1945—Juvenile literature.
Classification: LCC DD256.3 (ebook) | LCC DD256.3 .D58 2018 (print) | DDC
    940.53/1—dc23

LC record available at https://lccn.loc.gov/2017010790

Manufactured in the United States of America
1-43465-33205-6/14/2017

CONTENTS

INTRODUCTION
TEENAGE TERROR

Eighteen-year-old Simone Segouin stayed low. It was July 1944, and she was hiding in a ditch with two fellow French **resistance** fighters. World War II (1939–1945) raged across Europe, and **Nazi** Germany had taken over her home country of France.

Nazi German soldiers take over Paris, France, on June 14, 1940.

The **occupation** left many feeling helpless. Not Segouin. She was fighting back.

Under the false name Nicole Minet, she had joined the Free-Shooters and Partisans (*Francs-Tireurs et Partisans* in French, or FTP). The FTP was a group of resistance fighters. Their goal was to harm the occupying Germans and to drive them from France.

Segouin's missions with the FTP had started out small. She stole a bike from a German officer. She used it to deliver messages to other resistance fighters and spy on German troops. Over time, she proved her value to the FTP. She trained in **combat**. She carried out **sabotage** missions. Her aim was to damage German military posts and supply lines.

On that July morning, Segouin clutched her weapon as two German bicycles approached. Suddenly, she and her fellow fighters rose. She had never killed anyone in her life. But she didn't hesitate. Segouin opened fire. She wished that she didn't have to kill the enemy soldiers. But she also was willing to do whatever it took to defeat the enemy that had taken over her country.

Three members of the FTP, including eighteen-year-old Simone Segouin (*center*), prepare to fight German troops in Paris in 1944.

Maquis (*pictured*) were French resistance fighters in rural areas.

Segouin went on to become a legend among French resistance fighters. She helped in the capture of twenty-five German soldiers. She marched by the side of resistance leader Charles de Gaulle in the battle to recapture Paris. And she became a symbol of the resistance fighters that helped turn the tide of the war. She and countless others like her were not part of any official military. But these resistance fighters took up arms across Europe and did all they could to help defeat the enemy forces that threatened their countries.

CHAPTER 1
ACTS OF SABOTAGE

The Axis powers—Nazi Germany and its allies—spread across much of Europe during World War II. Using their military strength, they marched into nearby nations and took power. Life in an Axis-occupied nation was difficult. The Nazis were often brutal. They killed men and assaulted women. Children went hungry as enemy soldiers took most of the food.

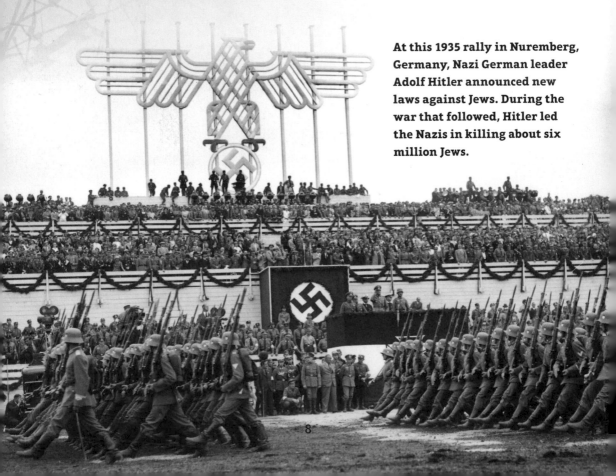

At this 1935 rally in Nuremberg, Germany, Nazi German leader Adolf Hitler announced new laws against Jews. During the war that followed, Hitler led the Nazis in killing about six million Jews.

Europe during World War II

NORTH
ATLANTIC
OCEAN

GREAT
BRITAIN

NORWAY

SWEDEN

DENMARK

HOLLAND

NETHERLANDS

SOVIET UNION

N

BELGIUM

GERMANY

POLAND

FRANCE

AUSTRIA

HUNGARY

SWITZERLAND

SPAIN

Miles
0   100   200   300

0   200   400
Kilometers

Many people felt powerless. Others were determined
to drive the enemy out. Usually they didn't have the
numbers or the weapons to fight back directly. So
many turned to sabotage. Their goal was to damage
enemy equipment and supply lines. They would make
life as hard as possible for the invaders.

MINOR SABOTAGE

In 1939 the Nazis invaded Poland. They plastered the city of Warsaw with posters that blamed Britain for the invasion. Student Elzbieta Zahorska protested by tearing down a poster. The Nazis responded by sentencing her to death.

It may have seemed like a small action. But Zahorska's protest was one of the earliest in a growing movement in Poland. It was called minor sabotage. Ordinary citizens carried out small acts designed to make life difficult for the Germans. They gave incorrect directions to German soldiers. They painted anti-Nazi graffiti. They pretended not to understand German when soldiers asked for help.

GETTING ORGANIZED

Small resistance bands began growing in occupied nations. In Denmark sixteen-year-old Knud Pedersen led a group of teenage boys who called themselves the Churchill Club. The young men used gasoline and matches to blow up Nazi vehicles. They stole weapons and destroyed airplane parts. In 1942 they were arrested and jailed. But even then, they escaped from their cells to carry out more acts of sabotage.

Other groups were organizing throughout Europe. In France the FTP became a constant thorn in the sides of the Axis forces. The Home Army in Poland grew to an estimated four hundred thousand.

Knud Pedersen (*back row, far right*) and the rest of the teenage Churchill Club were angry that their government had peacefully let the Nazis take over Denmark.

THINKING BIG

As German forces marched into the Soviet Union (a former nation made up of fifteen modern-day countries, including Russia), **civilians** worked to slow them at every step. On July 30, 1943, a resistance fighter attached an explosive to a fuel car at a busy train station. The massive explosion engulfed an ammunition car. It created a blaze that destroyed four trains. No one knows who set the explosion. Historians believe that it was a railway worker.

To get past the German guarding the SS *Donau*, Norwegian resistance members Max Manus and Roy Nielsen pretended to slip on ice on the shipyard dock. The guard laughed, and the distraction worked.

Norway became famous for its saboteurs. One of the most successful was Max Manus, who helped organize the Norwegian resistance movement. His specialty was in sinking German ships. In his most famous act, Manus and fellow resistance fighter Roy Nielsen used **mines** to destroy the German cargo ship SS *Donau*.

STEM HIGHLIGHT

Max Manus's tool of choice for blowing up ships was the limpet mine (*pictured*). This explosive device is attached to magnets.

A swimmer would dive underwater to stick a limpet mine to the **hull** of a ship. Compartments of air inside the mine made it buoyant. So it didn't just sink if the diver dropped it. Some limpet mines had small turbines attached. The mines wouldn't explode until the spinning blades had rotated enough times so that the ship had left the harbor.

CHAPTER 2
KNOWLEDGE IS POWER

Many resistance fighters spied on the Axis powers. They passed key **intelligence** along to the Allies, the countries that were fighting the Nazis. The information was crucial. It helped the Allies plan attacks, including the 1944 invasion of Normandy, France.

Allied troops bring supplies to Omaha Beach on June 8, 1944, during the Battle of Normandy.

COURIERS

Communication in the 1940s was difficult. Enemies could intercept radio signals. Codes could be broken. The Allies often relied on **couriers** to safely carry information to and from resistance groups behind enemy lines.

Polish-born Krystyna Skarbek was one of the best couriers. She pretended to be a journalist in Hungary. She used her cover to shuttle information from resistance fighters to the British military. Once, Italian soldiers stopped Skarbek. They ordered her to put her

Krystyna Skarbek
after the war ended

hands up. Skarbek lifted her arms to show them two
grenades with the pins pulled. She threatened to drop
the explosives and kill them all. The Italians ran for
their lives, leaving her free to carry on with her work.

SPIES

Daring resistance spies gathered intelligence on
the enemy. Working for the British, Lise de Baissac
parachuted into France. She posed as a poor widow. She

befriended German officers. She even rented a room in a house used by a German commander. The whole time, she kept her eyes and ears open for information that could be used against the Germans.

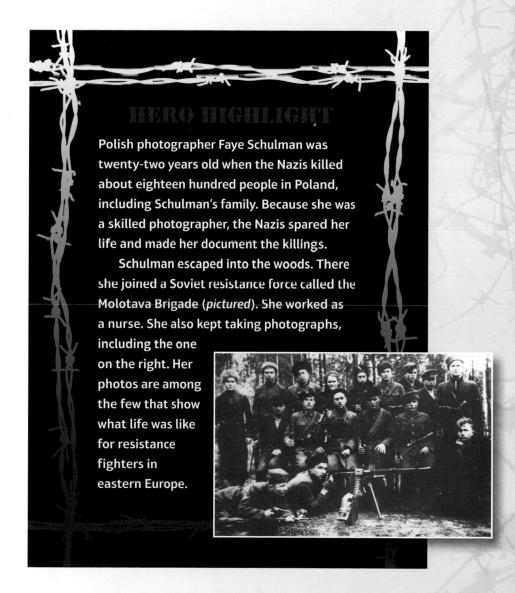

HERO HIGHLIGHT

Polish photographer Faye Schulman was twenty-two years old when the Nazis killed about eighteen hundred people in Poland, including Schulman's family. Because she was a skilled photographer, the Nazis spared her life and made her document the killings.

Schulman escaped into the woods. There she joined a Soviet resistance force called the Molotava Brigade (*pictured*). She worked as a nurse. She also kept taking photographs, including the one on the right. Her photos are among the few that show what life was like for resistance fighters in eastern Europe.

CHAPTER 3
RESCUE OPERATIONS

Europe was a dangerous place during World War II. The Nazis were carrying out a terrible **Holocaust**. They were rounding up Jewish people, as well as other groups, putting them into concentration camps, and killing them. About six million Jews were murdered. But that number could have been higher if not for dangerous rescue efforts.

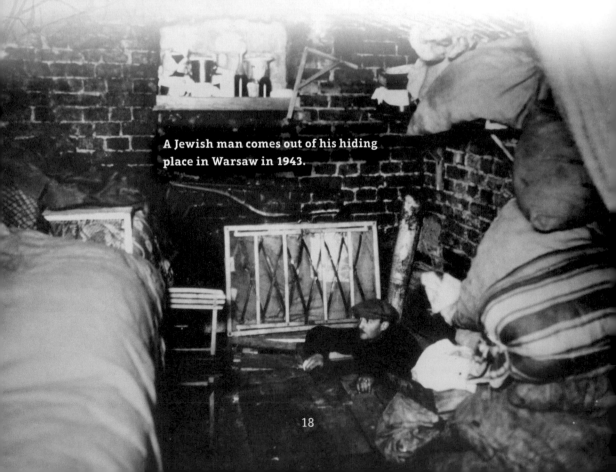

A Jewish man comes out of his hiding place in Warsaw in 1943.

Annie and Bert Bochove with their children, Eric (*center*) and Marise

Civilians hid Jewish people from the Nazis, often for years. They helped smuggle them to safe countries. And they did it all knowing it could cost them their lives if they were discovered.

In Holland, Bert and Annie Bochove ran a drugstore in a small town near Amsterdam. They were shocked as the Nazis started rounding up Jews, many of whom were their friends. The Bochoves added secret rooms to their house to hide dozens of Jews. Despite several close calls, the Germans never caught them or the people they saved.

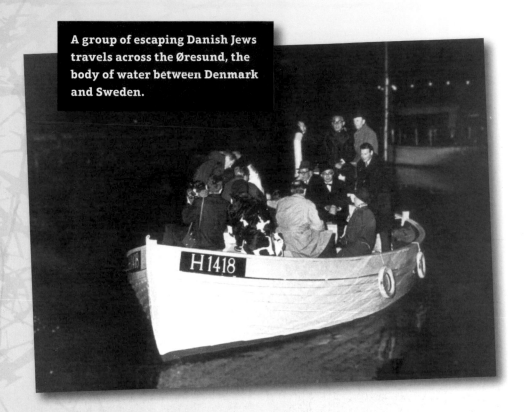

A group of escaping Danish Jews travels across the Øresund, the body of water between Denmark and Sweden.

In 1943 citizens of Denmark carried out one of the biggest rescue operations of the war. They received a tip that the Germans would be rounding up the nation's Jews. Almost overnight, the people of Denmark got more than seven thousand people into hiding. Over several days, the Dutch resistance smuggled most of them to neutral Sweden on fishing boats.

SAVING ALLIED SOLDIERS

Allied airmen and soldiers accidentally stuck behind enemy lines relied on resistance movements to return to safety. When Allied planes were shot down over the Netherlands, farmers such as the Mulder family hid the airmen from the Germans. "I stayed [at the Mulder house] for three months," recalled US B-17 pilot Ed Pollock. "They were wonderful people, and they risked their lives for us."

Large networks grew to help airmen and soldiers return to their jobs. Belgian resistance fighter Andrée de Jongh created the Comet line. This was a long network of safe houses that stretched from Brussels, Belgium, to neutral Spain. Guides helped airmen and soldiers follow the secret path to safety. The Comet line rescued about eight hundred Allied airmen and soldiers.

The Boeing B-17G was one model from the B-17 line, nicknamed the Flying Fortress. This plane featured thirteen guns and four engines.

CHAPTER 4
RISING UP

Resistance fighters didn't stop at indirect action.
They also took up arms and fought the Axis powers
directly. Some resistance groups targeted and killed
key Axis leaders.

Italian leader Benito Mussolini
(*far left*), Hitler (*center front*), and
other officials examine damage
at Nazi headquarters caused by
German resistance fighters.

Claus von Stauffenberg

The biggest plot was an attempt to kill Nazi Germany's leader Adolf Hitler. German military official Claus von Stauffenberg was troubled by the Nazis' treatment of Jews. He believed Hitler was leading Germany to ruin. He and other senior German leaders hatched a plot on Hitler's life.

The attempt to kill Hitler was international news. This front page from London's *Daily Herald* describes the attack.

It almost worked. The plan, called Operation Valkyrie, was carried out on July 20, 1944. Stauffenberg placed a briefcase loaded with a bomb beneath a table Hitler was using. However, someone else moved the briefcase before it exploded. Hitler suffered only minor injuries.

OPENING FIRE

Underground forces in France, Poland, and other nations grew tens or even hundreds of thousands strong. France's resistance forces, led by Charles de Gaulle, delivered one of the most storied victories in the war. De Gaulle led French forces into the nation's capital in August 1944. The French forces, which

French civilians prepare to fight German forces during the liberation of Paris on August 25, 1944.

French citizens celebrate defeating
the Germans in Paris in August 1944.

included young freedom fighter Simone Segouin, drove
the Germans from Paris. It was a major defeat to the
Nazis and a key event in turning the tide of the war.

The Allies—with resistance forces by their side—
recaptured France. They marched into Germany. On
April 30, 1945, as the Battle of Berlin raged around
him, Hitler took his own life. The war in Europe was

effectively over. And without the work of countless resistance fighters, the Germans might not have been defeated. The actions of resistance fighters, from small acts of disobedience to full-blown combat, were a key element in weakening and defeating Hitler's forces.

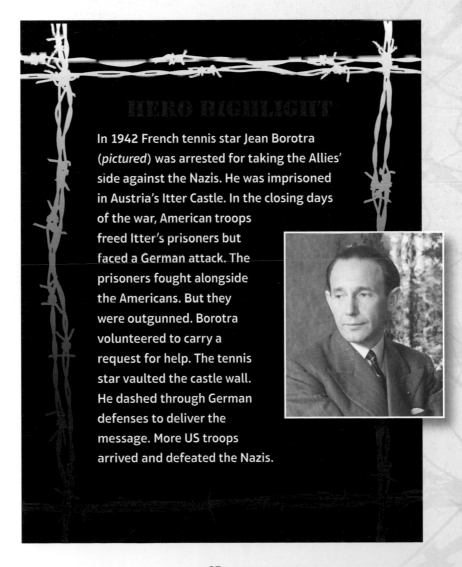

HERO HIGHLIGHT

In 1942 French tennis star Jean Borotra (*pictured*) was arrested for taking the Allies' side against the Nazis. He was imprisoned in Austria's Itter Castle. In the closing days of the war, American troops freed Itter's prisoners but faced a German attack. The prisoners fought alongside the Americans. But they were outgunned. Borotra volunteered to carry a request for help. The tennis star vaulted the castle wall. He dashed through German defenses to deliver the message. More US troops arrived and defeated the Nazis.

September 1, 1939	The German Nazis invade Poland. World War II begins.
June 14, 1940	The Germans enter Paris.
September 1942	Lise de Baissac parachutes into France. She poses as a poor widow while spying on German officers.
July 30, 1943	An unknown resistance fighter destroys multiple trains in the Soviet Union, greatly damaging German supply lines.
September 1943	The people of Denmark hide most of the nation's Jews and smuggle them aboard fishing boats to safety in Sweden.
July 20, 1944	Operation Valkyrie is launched. German military official Claus von Stauffenberg plants an explosive to kill Adolf Hitler. But Hitler receives only minor injuries.
August 1944	Charles de Gaulle leads French resistance fighters in the liberation of Paris.
January 1945	Max Manus uses limpet mines to destroy the SS *Donau*.

April 30, 1945   As the Battle of Berlin rages around him, Adolf Hitler takes his own life.

May 5, 1945   In the battle for Itter Castle, Jean Borotra makes a daring charge through German defenses to bring a message to US troops.

May 7, 1945   Germany formally surrenders, ending the European campaign of World War II.

Source Note

21 Bette McDevitt, "Tiny Mulder: Teenage World War II Resistance Heroine," *World War II*, November 2003, available online at *HistoryNet.com*, http://www.historynet.com/tiny-mulder -teenage-world-war-ii-resistance-heroine.htm.

Glossary

civilians: people who are not part of the armed forces or the police

combat: fighting between armed forces

couriers: people who carry and deliver messages or packages

Holocaust: the killing of about six million Jews and millions of others by Nazi Germany during World War II

hull: the main body of a ship

intelligence: strategic information about an enemy or the enemy's plans

mines: small explosives used either at or belowground or at water level

Nazi: a political party led by Adolf Hitler that ruled Germany from 1933 to 1945

occupation: the forceful taking over of another nation

resistance: a secret organization in a conquered country that fights back against the conquering country

sabotage: an act of damaging an enemy's property or slowing an enemy's mission

FURTHER INFORMATION

BBC: World War 2
http://www.bbc.co.uk/schools/primaryhistory/world_war2/

Byers, Ann. *Rescuing the Danish Jews: A Heroic Story from the Holocaust.* Berkeley Heights, NJ: Enslow, 2011.

Ducksters: World War II
http://www.ducksters.com/history/world_war_ii/

Freedman, Russell. *We Will Not Be Silent: The White Rose Student Resistance Movement That Defied Adolf Hitler.* Boston: Clarion Books, 2016.

Kallen, Stuart A. *World War II Spies and Secret Agents.* Minneapolis: Lerner Publications, 2018.

National Geographic Kids: 10 Eye-Opening Facts about World War 2
http://www.ngkids.co.uk/history/world-war-two

Otfinoski, Steven. *World War II.* New York: Children's Press, 2017.

United States Holocaust Memorial Museum
https://www.ushmm.org/

INDEX

PHOTO ACKNOWLEDGMENTS

The images in this book are used with the permission of: iStockphoto.com/akinshin, (barbed wire backgrounds throughout); iStockphoto.com/ElementalImaging, p. 1 (camouflage background); dpa picture alliance/Alamy Stock Photo, pp. 4–5; Hulton Deutsch/Corbis Historical/Getty Images, p. 6; Pictorial Press Ltd/Alamy Stock Photo, pp. 7, 28; Sueddeutsche Zeitung Photo/Alamy Stock Photo, p. 8; © Laura Westlund/ Independent Picture Service, p. 9; AP Photo/Julien Bryan, p. 10; Churchill Club/ Wikimedia Commons (CC BY-SA 4.0), pp. 11, 29 (left); Photograph by Walter E. Frost/ Courtesy the City of Vancouver Archives, p. 12; The National Archives/Wikimedia Commons (Open Government License v1.0), p. 13; National Archives (SC 193082), p. 14; INTERFOTO/Alamy Stock Photo, p. 15; Trinity Mirror/Mirrorpix/Alamy Stock Photo, p. 16; iStockphoto.com/aaron007, pp. 17, 27 (barbed wire frame); United States Holocaust Memorial Museum, courtesy of Belarusian State Museum of the History of the Great Patriotic War, pp. 17, 29 (right); United States Holocaust Memorial Museum, courtesy of National Archives and Records Administration, College Park, p. 18; United States Holocaust Memorial Museum courtesy of Rescuers: Portraits of Moral Courage in the Holocaust, p. 19; AFP/Getty Images, p. 20; US Air Force Photo, p. 21; akg-images/Alamy Stock Photo, p. 22; picture alliance/dpa/Newscom, p. 23; John Frost Newspapers/Alamy Stock Photo, p. 24; National Museum of the US Navy, p. 25; US Army via CNP/Newscom, p. 26; Keystone-France/Getty Images, p. 27.

Cover: Keystone-France/Getty Images (resistance fighters); iStockphoto.com/akinshin (barbed wire background); iStockphoto.com/ElementalImaging (camouflage background); iStockphoto.com/MillefloreImages (flag background).